PRAISE FOR *THE JOURNEYMEN*:

"In a bar in Little Rock, I listen to a poet reciting his own work and nod my head at the cadence. The man beside me asks me if I know any poems for truck drivers these days.

" 'Take a look at Pablo Neruda,' I tell him. 'There maybe D.A. Powell and yes, James Jay.'

" 'James Jay?'

"So I tell him about James Jay and his new book, *The Journeymen*. Find I can actually remember some of the 'letter from the united states department of poetry' and then most of 'The Briefly Unemployed Bouncer'. "His mind is an '83 Dodge Colt." My new friend laughs and nods. He once owned a Dodge Colt. His was unreliable.

"If I could, I would give him the whole of 'Mountain Rivera' but I know I would start to cry at the story—a life that echoes the men in my family as starkly as the flattened planes of their aging faces.

"*The Journeymen* is that rare thing—a book as meaty as its subjects, as thick as silence, and as satisfying as a perfect blues riff."

—Dorothy Allison, author of *Bastard Out of Carolina*

The Journeymen

by James Jay

The Journeymen

by James Jay

For Maddy,

" Poetry is a weapon loaded with the future!"

Thanks for the hospitality.

James

GORSKY PRESS
LOS ANGELES • CALIFORNIA
2010

Minneapolis 7/9/2010

Published by
Gorsky Press
P.O. Box 42024
Los Angeles, CA 90042

copyright © 2010 by James Jay
all rights reserved

ISBN 0-9753964-9-8

cover painting
"I Remember This One Time"
by Kiyoshi Nakazawa

cover design
by Sean Carswell

for Alyson

Table of Contents

III. Thunderhats

IV. The Pints

V. The United States Department of Poetry

Time Trapped in Light

I'm about at the point
       in the season
where I'm ready to mine
       this writing journal.
The pages left
       are few. The year
           comes to an end.
I have
       some spare time.
           The signs are good.

In my desk drawer I've found
a photo of my old pal,
Jack Kerouac, tuning a radio.

In it he's just landed
on the magic frequency:
       a basketball game,
           a boxing match,
               a Zoot Simms melody,
           some Jazz not known
               to any of us.
Hard to say which.

His eyes closed; fingers
       moving ever so slightly
back, successful

in their caresses; cheeks
softly slanting down; hair
        black, a big tuft of it clumped together
                as if combed by a fist;
the ridge of his brow solid,
        that sweet
                frequency gathered
into the back of that brow,
        piling up back there.

Those years and years of searching
        for those notes
and here we are
        smack dab
                in the middle of it:
fifty years of History
        and a black & white still keeps
                me in Jack's tune,
that tune, so wonderfully lost
        in that time:

                Wooden desk, sprinkled
                        with drill bits and an empty
                                glass jar.
                Wire running up
                        to a shelf
                                not attached
                to anything I can see.
                Everything else,
                        everything else,
                                just so much light & time,

so much stellar humming,
         reflection,
                  star dust refracting.

                  I could weep all night long
         content, ecstatic
in this big, big universe!

— Flagstaff, Arizona 12/12/06

I.
Creosote

What Her Grandfather Gave Her

In the garage the child
      has a wooden block
           she painted blue
from the left over
      wedgewood
           that went the way
of the fence posts.
      There's enough
           of the mustard yellow
from the cabinets
      to give
           a feeling of depth.

So she does
      with tiny paintbrushes
           from trim work
found
      in the buckets left
           last winter.
Now, she has
      a hammer and beats
           time on the block.
The nails are kept
      by her grandpa
           for safety's sake

on the counter
      her handful of years

can't quite reach.
She smacks and smacks,
    as if the concept
        of square, of round
are notes that need
    a good whack
        in order to sing —

Mars Hill

for Alyson

That night-hike up Mars
Hill, a flask of John Powers going
down fast, my finger brushing
your hand on the exchange,
big full moon, and light-rain
that morphed to sheets
of snow as we climbed
to the log where we found
ourselves a seat.

              You leaning in
to kiss me, me too scared to go
first, wet lips, snow drenched
faces and heads, followed by the firm hold
of hands as we leapt back down
the trail like

            Jack & Jill: the tale revised
as if by dumb angels who scribbled sweet,
naïve edits with no flare
for drama; simply stupid enough
to wish to help; who worked
the soles of our feet to keep us
from falling familiarly down; who erased twisted
ankles; who brushed aside sticks, stones;
kept our shoes tied; our strides in step.
The angels whose pens are filled
with the ink of surviving

               so many

falls before, the dumb angels

that earned the calluses that guide
us; the light of stars caught
in the scars of their barely visible cheeks!

In Los Angeles
for Jim Jay

Blind now, my father works his way
along the sidewalks
with thousands of the protesters
of this war, the last war, the next one.

Now, he only wears his uniform
for these ceremonies;
101st Airborne, purple heart with cluster,
bronze star, a lot of metal on his chest,

the white cane and black sunglasses
enlisted in the ensemble.
He's lost his sight just this year.
The flare in his face in the Vietnam

of decades ago taxed the rods and cones and now
time knocks out the rest of the spectrum.
Still, he manages to march
against this war, the last war, the next one.

The younger than 30 protesters speak loudly
at him with thank yous and search
to find his hand to shake. He smiles
and speaks a few words there and here.

The young, myself included at times,
know nothing beyond the uniform and cane.

They see what they're going to see.
For all they know

his eyes were plucked from him in the era
Titans ran the show, and he's gone on
fighting, cloaked in the simplifications of heroism.
An old story that could go however you like, then …

Then, the crowd finally begins
        to bend, to get to business. He marches.
                The people spill

into the streets, parking lots,
        city parks. Narratives drop
            to the concrete.

They march. The wind smells
        of sea water.
                Satiated, it pours

around him as if
        pounding into a tired boulder
            that won't go away,

that won't go along
        with the program of erosion
and what comes next.

A Letter from the United States Department of Poetry
for Robert Jay

Comrades, my belly full of guilty food,
I sit in a comfortable chair
in an apartment with a strong winter's draft,
but not so many leaks.

I read of our patriarch, Pablo Neruda,
writing of his brothers in the mines
where they wear masks of coal.
They toil in hell and with fists and forearms,
with pick and hammer they bang
their way into his poems: a remembrance
of their fire in the face of such cold depths.

This is the scope, the breath of Don Pablo.
But for me, I confess, I've never been so big,
the family of my heart so wide.

For this evening the snow drifts
on the porch carry my brother's name;
over and over they blow about the same letters,
the same thoughts piling up.

For my own brother toils in a prison
in Orange County clocking-in
as a guard, full-time, for the medical benefits,
for the regular paycheck,
for the hope of escape.

To this end he works a second job
at night on the docks,
part-time, Longshoreman,
not yet Union, still in jeopardy
of being replaced by the generality
of machines and the O's and X's of soft CFO's.

Comrades, tonight all I can tell you
is of one sibling,
one who reads texts of twelfth century Chinese philosophers,
who knows more about Li Po than the next guy,
who grows thicker in his forearms and shoulders,
who wields poles and hooks,
who never complains,
for whom the moonlight
awaits each evening
on the sea,

the sweet moonlight the same
on our snow banks, on our rivers of ice,
there to illuminate,
to shine on
our hands' grand ambitions
for whoever
needs to see.

Ronald Reagan Killed my Band Teacher so Now I Can Never Play Backup for Huey Lewis or The News

You know how it goes.
On the bus they beat
the crap out of you for carrying
a band instrument, hard plastic shell
        and no breaks for anyone.

Me, I lugged the alto sax
that my mother, who worked
through robberies and drunk managers
at the grocery store, bought
        on payments.

I drug that woodwind
past bench seats and their dirty,
stuck bubble gum & graffiti,
each day, every day to sit in the classroom
        and play third chair.

Then, somewhere, a B-rate actor
was elected president, made ketchup
a vegetable, declared victory over Soviets
and their wooden missiles, and fired
        our soft spoken band leader

who left the classroom to walk home
to his living room and take
a revolver's bullet to his brain's

sad & tired muse, so that now
　　　　two decades past,

I sit by firelight, the woodstove
punching against the winter's weather
and I read & read and think
of those plastic chairs
　　　　in which I sat for months & months

the school's secretary at the room's main desk
scribbling into the long business checks,
filing forms and envelopes,
and shouting to us to shut up
　　　　and read FACE

and Every Good Boy Deserves Fudge
and quiet, quiet. My alto sax, the same type
as my talented Uncle
(the reason my mother picked it
　　　　for me to play)

the alto sax sitting in its hard shell,
a labored woodwind to eventually
fade, to vanish into that space
where we learn to shut up.
　　　　None of us knows where

these failed instruments go.
But, wouldn't we love to salvage
them, their beaten flat notes,
their compromised hopes of success
　　　　and the love of the moment

from which they sprang from our mother's minds,
that place impervious to budgets,
that carrying case
we can open to find
        a tune we can carry?

Someone Must Have Quit

Highway 89 —
      heading south.

A brown cowboy
      boot bent and sunning
in the middle
      of the road.

Sympathy for Jesus

At the wheel of the V.W. bug,
Jesus, short-legged, pot-bellied,
he rounds up the kids from the trailers
of Kingman, of Birdland, of Butler.

He sticks his hands out the window
into the scorching summer air
as the V.W. takes slow, wide turns
all on its own. "The hands of God

now have the wheel!
You better believe!"
the Jesus of the V.W. hollers.
We children scream and hoot. How can this be?

And my ten year old brain, even then, rushes
after answers, reasons that this is more about shouting
than Faith fighting off the Two-pronged
Devil of the Car Wrecks.

For the road is dirt, the speed slow,
the soft tumbleweeds of the desert pad
any lapses, a scraping of paint
seems the only concern: more desert landscaping.

It is as if Jesus wants us
on the road to protect the cacti, the creosote,
the stray rabbits, a dim-witted Gila Monster or two.

For this Jesus is kind, and I can't imagine

him harming us by car crash,
by asphalt, by God, by anything at all.
His shouting is merely contagious
like the noise of parents

in the creaking, white-washed bleachers
of a little league game
with an all dirt outfield:
noise scooping up more noise.

This scene, nonetheless, clings to my memory,
my mind. So what does that mean?
In the middle of the night, wrapped
in insomnia I return

to this rolling. We ride past the sleeping dogs
chained to stakes, that V.W. loaded
with six or seven children, ready to pop
like circus clowns coming for the last

of the well bourbon at Happy Hour.
And despite the friction
of sweaty, scrawny arms and shoulders,
the churching just doesn't stick,

after a few months I conclude V.W. Jesus
just steers with his fat knees, and the Jehovah's Witnesses
a desert block away, who eat pomegranates
and detest birthdays have a better chance

of converting Bozo The Clown, leaving me
in the end to try to make
meaning, a closing couplet,
out of reasoning,

for how could God stand an apple's chance
in a high desert climate?
Maybe He didn't take because He seemed foreign,
fragile, endangered, as difficult to comprehend

as forty-day floods; Beelzebub; a green, lavish garden;
the camel and the murderous eye of the needle;
the tongues in which He spoke revealed
God's stories *aint from around here.*

For who in America speaks in terms of camels?
And only my grandmother used sewing needles,
but I liked His boy, His Jesus of the V.W.,
who taught me more about deductive reasoning

than the Sherlock Holmes paperbacks,
who bestowed upon me a thirst
for knowledge that later plunged me
into Aristotle's great tomes.

And tonight I drink a shot of whiskey
to his teachings, to his example,
to his riled and rowdy words,
to the air on which his hands clenched.

Golems

In Kingman they're fleshed out
from creosote and fifty caliber bullets,
the copper that miners gave up on,
the ground water,
dirt clods and Russian Thistle,
plastic and abandoned asphalt,
devil's feet and goat heads,
barbed wire and dry fence posts,
bleached bones of cattle and coyotes,
the chains of long dead dogs, their discarded collars,
the arid wind
winding its tired way to you:

You, the architect of golems,
wringing Ambition's broken
and mended fingers —
cracked nails and eyes consuming
an adobe wall's
chicken wire supports
that shove through
what someone claimed as home.

II.
Rivera

The Tank Mechanic
for Tom Beggerow

"One learns survival by surviving."
— Charles Bukowski

The M48A1, the M60,
show him a machine
the Amtrac, the Ontos,
and its numbered name,
the M155, or M105,
charges to the tongue's tip.

Photos of the boy with no sense
of humor, or the one who lost
his leg to a Bouncing Betty
and things stall a bit.
His memory sputters & coughs.
A rank comes to mind.

The M48A1, the M60,
all keep the line in the Present,
the Amtrac, the Ontos,
and have held their ground
the M155, or M105
since they melted Marble Mountain —
its stones pouring, flowing, burying
a parade of lighted candles
and drops & drops of blood.

For more than thirty rotations

around the sun, he has banged
headlong into this wall.
"Tonight, there must be another way,"
he says. He walks out
onto his porch anchored

to the other side
of the planet, sips a brandy,
Asbach Uralt, from a snifter,
and reaches up into the night,
pauses,
stretches some more,

and he takes the moon
in his fingers and turns
it around like the handle
of a precision lathe
in a steel mill. Its craters
surprised at first to see him,

they all stare a while,
then he asks questions.
He listens to their refractions,
the lights of ten thousand candles
take notes in the shadows
under the swaying ponderosa pines —

Mountain Rivera

Mountain Rivera made it
most his career as an undercard,

broke into the top 20
on the World Boxing Conference rankings

once. Big Mountain never threw nothing
but big rights, gave it his all each punch,

each fight, and was offered plenty
to go down to the pretty & promoted boys.

But the Mountain never flopped, kept slugging,
lumbering forward in half steps.

He got a crack
at a kid who used to be

called Cassius Clay. And that was the end
of the Mountain.

This kid, Cassius, kept landing
jabs, jabs. Detached Rivera's retina,

broke his nose,
stubborn jaw, until in the tenth

from his trainer's hand the towel flew

like a shot grouse.

.

Later, Mountain cleaned up, covered himself
in a King-sized Italian suit, made

his half blind way
to the unemployment office

for a job, one that was "legit."
His paws too specialized for

construction & White Collar was a joke
where the funny landed on him.

Where was the drywall job
that could have saved him? Nothing.

So Mountain went to Rasslin,'
lost his Rivera somewhere

in a headdress of red
and white feathers fanning

all the way down to his ass, became
the promoter's "Injun," whoo hoo whoo hoo'd

his way into matches every night
where he'd be cowboy'd out of there,

hog tied, his pride flopping on the mat
like a fish in an old story

where we all know the hook
has been set. Still we all pull

for Mountain to make it. Don't we?
His pride a gift:

an unreasonable thought
in our head that if we stick and move

long enough our finest hour is ahead
of us, slugging its way into the bruised

and busted future. For the Mountain
is long gone from the ring

(boxing, 'Rasslin, or otherwise),
replaced by a guy named Rivera

who lives in the run-down shack of cliché,
whose 2" by 4"s are warped,

whose flooring complains
from each step we take across it,

whose shingles have been blown
onto the dead grass of the lawn.

But this, of course, is all the wood
and the steel and the concrete

of a good old fashioned Tragedy.
The only hitch —Mountain's no pug,

never was no Shakespearean bum.
He knows the fix is always in,

and the last thing he'd do is play
the Baby Face of a poem.

He looks in the smeared mirror and sees
the Hamlet his cousin acted

in high school performances in the gym.
He delivers fragments of soliloquies

he hasn't heard in decades. Interrupts himself
sometimes with the answers:

"Something is rotten in the ...
Oh, you're telling me? You're telling me?"

He goes on and on.
No one punched that blank verse

from his brain,
and he'd rather have iambs

than rent. So finally, he retires
to our thoughts

where his legs are agile as language:
the fix is always in, baby.

His arthritic fists swing
in looping arcs of thought:

the fix is always in,
as he just misses that newly

found uppercut
to the horizon's jagged profile.

Paradise, USA

for Emma

A store where they sell
second hand piñatas
and masking tape;
shoes chewed by a half coyote mutt;
broken zippers; recycled oil in the engine;
and urine with vitamin C;
busted handcuffs with no keys;
the rhetoric of the masses
and waxy ear plugs.

Reader, come by. Come by.
Let's talk about transmissions.

The School Teacher's Elegy

In Occupied Tibet the Chinese
school teacher assigns points
for killing.
>   A fly – one point
>   A worm – two
>   A mouse – five
>   A cat – ten
>   and so forth, and so on.

To smash quickly and finish or
to probe for numb spots, the children
consider how to compassionately crush
worms. Their conclusions fall on the soil.

One girl, early in the morning, guided
by the unblinking wind, pulls
her fly from a web: a desiccated triumph
the mountains won't snitch.

The boys and girls pour through
the classroom door with their flies.
Arriving late, an eight year old boy dressed
in the cold, chafing, fabric of fear

brings his dog, skull busted
by a stone surprised to find
what it would be up to for the afternoon
as the child lifted it quickly,

as if to toss across the dirt road for distance, then
didn't. This child has seen
his mother raped, watched soldiers
point his brother's hand loaded

with a pistol at their father and fire.
And from the ceiling of the world
this suffering trickles
down the river of economics

where Imperialism is carried like so much silt
pooling around your feet.
In this muck you might ask what do you get
for killing the damn teacher?

His Holiness the Dalai Lama would not.
Bring in your own head first, he might advise.
Take a dull blade to your neck and get to work.
Bring it with no more emotion than the masked

slasher of the American horror movies.
Who demanded points for parts from you?
Western science lost track of where
the soul sits in your body, so

offer them your appendix as a decoy.
Can you lament the school teacher
who offered the dwarf god of security
his compassion, tossed out like

worn engine parts at the end of a job?
The dwarf god stretches up,

staples grey scales to the school
teacher's supple skin; attaches

yellow claws with the thick, bent spikes of fear;
chisels his canines so sharp he bites
his lower lip when he speaks in any language
other than the guttural, slow-jawed jargon of jingoism.

Look around your feet, and this god
looks back from below, beckoning you to leap.
In a class filled with the dead, this satisfied,
this suited teacher tells how Mao

came to liberate the people of Tibet.
Who has spoken to you of liberation lately?
Who has asked you to snarl and bare it,
to scratch at your chest?

Skin and hair have already amassed
under yellowing nails. Take your chapped
and callused hands and bring them here.
Here, where you write

this poem for His Holiness the Dalai Lama.
Where you write this poem though
he won't read it. Where you write
this poem simply

              because you are a lover of his name.

Today Let's Call Ourselves Ghalib

You might as well be God
        or Ghalib —
There's no other choice, the either or
        fallacy is all your brain
                stem feels this morning.

So let's be Ghalib, if only for
        today. That's more fun —
Ghalib. As Ghalib, you gather up early
        in life that decay constantly

coming off each beast, each tree, each
        plant. You place it in a torn pocket, your lunch
pail, stash it in Ziploc bags in a freezer for later —
        the philosophy of detritus you master quickly.

With your mother you rub tombstones
        in the graveyard by your childhood
house. She wants to teach you of
        pioneers, your past. Later

you research the found names on that charcoal
        sketched paper, match the design to the county library
records, the etchings on forms in files wherever you find
        them. Those words as frightening as

ghosts, always come back to you, disturbed,
        ageless, unshakeable. Is this when

Ghalib's favorite fantasy had to do
            with Heaven? He knows only

paper and charcoal, but Heaven is his
            favorite fantasy: Heaven — where
the pioneers go, where words go when
            they finally come to terms

with their meaning, their tired context.
            So Ghalib becomes a photographer or
a poet. I don't recall what you exactly
            did. (How strange you are today, Ghalib!)

After all, all I work with is
            your imagery.
You take the fore-arms
            of the bride

on her wedding day and remove them.
            She still looks at the unencumbered
horizon with hope. Would her husband be
            as cheery, if he knew you

and your trespass, your desire? You take the factory
            worker girl at the cotton mill, drop
the V-line of her filthy blouse
            a few inches. Still she goes back

to work for her pennies a day.
            You go on and on.
Captain's daughters sleep alongside
            their rotting salmon.

Your best friend reveals scars that
            you erase. Your Jesus
touches himself to prove his faith
            to you, a paradoxical prick

at your command. You tape
            a binocular lens to your 35mm
and snap skin. You define arroyo
            as a cleft in the brain.

Ghalib, dig up that cougar your father
            buried at the beginning of summer.
He wants to teach you about
            biology. Go find that corpse,

less cleanly picked
            than his science
had predicted. Let the color come
            into your cheeks —

You might as well be Ghalib.
            You might as well call down
the sky. So tasty the air
            when you fill

your lungs all at once!

This Is It, This Is It

A man squats in the hull of your language, tapping
on the planks with a carpenter's hammer. "End
it now," he mutters. "End it now." He just wants
to let the sea into your life. Flush you out a bit.

The Captain is in no hurry, however, to finish
his lunch. He knows about the konks. But, the sailors
caught and prepped some deep down fish, gone astray,
just for the plate. Someone will be dispatched

in time. The hammer will give up on its handle.
Or the sailors will fix the shackles before
the evening news. Who knows? So many things go
right that hardly anything is worth planning.

It's Tuesday and nothing ever floods on Tuesdays.
What were your ports of call? The flag tattoo
on your shoulder blew away years ago.
You're just visiting. Cruising some American sounds.

At the other end of the table your host, Gentry,
rubs his bald skull, leans his meaty arm down to brace
himself. He reads philosophy or is it another
men's magazine? Foucault is this month's centerfold.

By candlelight it's hard to guess
his stats, his hobbies, his pet peeves.

Baelnablath

But he behaved himself,
already cowed
by the nightsticks that left him alone.
                — Larry Levis

Closed to your knocks
            on the front door,
the house that reads
            PUB opens
from behind. An old man,
            could be your father,
could be Cuchulainn back
            from his defeat
by the sea, this old man
            waves a thick, jacketed
arm in the rain and points
            you to the fence
in back of your expectations.

A nod for thanks
            in the air,
in the damp, and you're in
            the yard, German
Shepherd wagging
            so much furred joy.
Pat its agitated wet head,
            awkwardly. The best
you can do is pick
            someone's home to try,

so you do; you, the failed journeyman
        of a fistful of trades.
Go ahead again,
        rely on luck —

Anthracite and Murphy's await
        you, along with Tom,
a lanky pub keeper,
        negotiator of countless schisms
over Paddy's
        and John Powers.
Turn the knob on the back door
        and push.
What you wouldn't give
        to not compromise?
This is my broken nose,
        and I'll take another.

Of course, this is why
        you're here.
Your nose was
        busted a number
of times, years ago, until
        the cartilage solidified
and in its hardening
        and bent longing
another option mended:
        credit, a loan of some
sorts, for a smile a girl
        spotted you bus fare —

In one tolerated piece

you've come to see
the memorial to Michael Collins,
which you know better
than to ask about,
for while your hero
is from here, here was finally
won by De Valera's
voice. So who killed
your desire?
Was it the Brits? Imperialists?
Was it your own
guards? A foreign plant? Tom wants
to say yes to the latter
more than he wants
whiskey, more than peace.
What if it were
one of your own? Your Irregulars
who won't even listen
to Dev or Brits or demons
of any sorts?

You know of the crane
who became king
and devoured all the fish
in the pond who
entitled him; still, you climb
the path to the knoll.
An old man's life later
that lead won't fly
any truer to your heart's
bulls-eye. Climb
that knoll and dig

in the bushes,
under the rocks,
        scrape the moss,
scout the trees.

Let your fingers numb
        with knowledge.
Pivot from worn boot
        to boot.
This ambush is blown.
        It's too late in the day.
Opt not to take the shot.

Slosh out of the way,
        up the muddy road
to the north, slip along
        to that tavern
where they make the best
        lunch in the county.
Feed your body fried
        anything and feel
warm again, boast about
        your business and
swallow that fist
        (coming right your reckless
way) with your face.

Dawn Patrol

Grey light.
The sun yawns
its way into the sky.

The industrious hobo, skinny;
skinny legs in thin, thin jeans;
black sweatshirt with hood over his head,

roams the sidewalk
across the street from me —
For blocks we share the same pace.

Trash can to trash can he prowls —
no potential passed.
We patrol our sides.

I take my cue and won't pass up
this sign, this good fortune
from toiling bones and flesh!

I fall in love with the cigarette butts
      in the gutter,
            the last lips to call them theirs,
      before the cast off;

the broken glass
      done with being
            of use to anyone;

the plastic bag
     becoming
         the wind's art
     on the canvas of air —

III.
Thunderhats

The Fourth of July County Fair Donkey Speaks

I'm no merry go round.
I'm no merry go round.

I wish I were
a carnivore,
then for the sheer love
of teeth I'd snap
that red, white, and blue wearing
girl off the back
of my brother chained
before my nostrils,

and he'd bite the one
before him,
and she before her,
until it came around
in one great proletarian loop
where this kicking creature
screaming on my back
digests in the ulcer lined stomach
of History.

Oh canines, what sweet, sweet teeth,
so unsatisfied by cake!

Pulling Down the Sky:
A Report Prepared for President Bush

This morning at the county jail,
after the 4th metal door
and before the 5th and 6th,
we walk through the general, non-
violent population: some
shackled standing, waiting;
some leaning into the Navajo
white walls; some mopping;
some sweeping. Most are happy
to say hello, to talk about what
we're doing (giving a poetry reading),
where we're going (juveniles convicted
as adults wing), friendly enough.

The smell, stale, thick
with breathed over and over air,
the noise, sudden: hammer
slam of metal on metal bars,
falling and falling through the halls;
yet, as a classroom it's not
so bad once a few lines emerge.

Why don't you come on by? Drop
in like a principal, some high up
administrator, lean in the back,
nod, nod, take some notes.
We won't ask you to write

on the chalkboard or solve
the bubbles with the number 2 pencil,
no standardized tricks. Just
lean and listen a bit.

Today's topic: Milarepa.
Milarepa, 11th Century Tibetan
Saint, conjured sheets of hail
over his uncle's crops after he
stole Milarepa's familial lands,
then finished the uncle
by chanting a ceiling onto
his head at church. His words:
black magic. His fear: a storm
of rats. He was young, smart, quick
with his tongue, scared and had time
on his hands.

This was 1000 years ago and he's reformed
now. No need to serve him
a Patriot Act Protection Order,
or some such thing. He turned his powers,
his dark words,
into poetry to save his Karma,
to contain himself, to get his
shit together.

Hardworking student, A.J.,
taps his right foot, covered with a white sock,
and plastic slipper, on the concrete floor.
He is reminded of last week's lesson;
he digs through his torn sheets of paper,

and reads some of Czeslaw Milosz's
thoughts on poets: *In a culture busy*
with getting food, survival, a poet
found a place as witch-doctor,
shaman, possessor of spells
which protect, cure, or harm.

At county jails, jailed citizens pick
metaphors from the paint, gather imagery
with trembling fingers,
horde rhythm and meter
in their empty stomachs.
Mr. President we'd rather keep
our Karma in tact. Let's talk.
I know you're not big
on subtlety, so here it goes:
you're fucking with the children
of Milarepa, you're fucking
with the wrong guys.
Put this in your FBI file.

Crazy Joe

In the grocery store
by the milk
and heading toward
the beer
and liquor,
I spot
Crazy Joe
coming.

He launches
a lime
right into the center
of my gut,

then charges,
long-legged
over the linoleum,
through the distance,
with a lanky
hug
closing down
the space
in which to hit him.

He hugs,
laughs
and howls.
Crazy Joe

right here
at the end of my day
of accountants,
attorneys,
and bankers.

Tall, strong,
he wraps
his arm
over my shoulders
and walks me
by the cheeses
and herring cans
bathed in the light
of fluorescent bulbs.
"Have you met my gal?"
he asks.

Of course,
I never know,
having met plenty
of girls
that go with Joe.

Steely Dan crackles
on the store speakers;
he tugs me to her
past my day
of accountants,
attorneys,
and bankers.
Pushed past

aisles and aisles,
my belly button
blotted
with a wet
circle of
possibilities
stinging —

Embraced in the Spider Web

for Cesar, a poet who gave me this title

Is it loyalty that holds you tight as black
gripping the grass on the lawn at night?
Embraced in the spider web, embraced
the way that bad news woman holds you at night.

How irresistible those thin, tattooed arms,
and shaky, hands. Those hands that
hurl things, that ball up in a tiny fist,
that bring drinks, incessantly, to those red,

red, redder than life lips. Embraced:
that stickiness, that more you struggle
dilemma, the more spread out you
get with each smooth strand.

Is it loyalty, the raw physics of its friction,
that holds you? Habit's cold, indifferent, inertia?
Is it insecurity's draw, its gravity that keeps you falling
into an orbit of trouble? Is there a difference?

And this, of course, deals with love, so let's
apply some science. Premise A: your house
leaks, pull up the ceiling tiles and you find
grand stalactites running down your pipes;

the toilet, propped on 2" x 4"s, bolted down
now more by rust than metal; pliers permanently

parked on the side of the tub
for the missing hot water handle.

Tell your friends to come over and you need
to give them directions, warnings, on how to do
their daily business. So loaded with allegory,
your house, that its trusses strain to support

your dreams at night.
When you sleep, your lips softly murmur,
"I'll live with what's left.
I'll live…"

Premise 2: embraced in strands and strands
of the day to day. Let's call that stressed.
Stressed as Randy, inmate, 17 years old, going on
to the Darkside (as he calls it) in a week

where it'll be tough to turn in his poem,
his homework he does. His lawyer calls
in the middle of class and he has to take the phone
and moves from the world of poetry.

"Just pick it off. One at a time." I heard
once. Was it Coach Axe Handles hollering
in the wrestling room, the humidity
and the heat and fatigue making Axe Handles

imminently wise? And what are you stressed about?
"Everything. All of it." says Randy.
Just keep picking off the pieces, the holds —
that headlock, that iron cross, that suplex, that chronic debt.

Stop picking off that pressure and boom!
That bad news woman, always back to one of those,
and she just left a bad news man you probably
have to deal with too. Maybe it's you all along.

Always back to that, dump her, send her
and her wall display kimonos, two closets of shoes,
furniture with upper-case names packing, and won't you be so
cold at night? Embraced by loneliness, nothing to follow,

and along came a spider and ... you know
how it goes from there? Something so simple

as a nursery rhyme soothes you in its narration
of fear, as if knowing the story's end
lets you fling a strand or two.
So premise A and premise 2 and for our conclusion

we dismiss the psychiatrist with his smoking jacket.
We dismiss him to dig a ditch, put his back
into it until his shovel finds a place where there's only
a dream and no waking, no sleeping. Dreams

ride on the top of dreams like one theory
of the universe: turtles stacked on top of turtles,
dull, claws on round thick paws scratching
on shell after shell like a constant whisper

until reality becomes the singing of turtles all the way down.
And we move the psychiatrist, his hands now callused
and his back aching, we move him into a house
where the morning light is so gorgeous he swears

it's holy, drops his explanations into Truth's wastebasket,
so much unopened junk mail,
and with such grace he finds
sculpture, maybe paints a bit, considers

working with a glass canvas, then does.
With a business card, he invites you in and you don't have to
take the invitation as anything more than
that. No need to ask for the meaning

of the tired font. No need to analyze how
the ticket taker in a polyester suit tears the stub
with wreckless abandon. And the boy, asks you
for your code and you press a red button

say "Cooze 497' into a speaker that hangs
from his neck and rests on his thin chest.
The boy, a bit of a blemish problem, the smell
of cheap deodorant and full-blown

adolescence says, "James Jay, you could have been
 a visionary, if only you didn't booze it up so much,
                if only you knew an embrace."

"Very Good Coffee I Might Add"

says the thin man whose arms
hang like a set of frayed climbing ropes.
They're so thin that when
the hands move back to the cup
you'd guess the waves of heat
would be too heavy.

He sips, says his
mouth is named Tomorrow;
his fingers Anxiety.
When he places them to
his mouth to signal hush
you find you won't
sleep again
for years.

His job is to give out jobs:
the nightmare with a task.
Do the dishes. Windex the windows.
So you do
and you do.
Still, the stars
won't come around
until he says so.

Marching Off to See The Prophet

It snowed three feet
of heavy, wide flakes

in the last twenty-four hours.
Streets froze.

Drivers noted rise
over run ratios.

An elm crashed
through the windshield

of my truck
that doesn't go

in this weather,
whether or not

a tree crashes on it.
The grocery store closed

before the grey sun
quit the day.

Downtown locked in ice,
the liquor store

hunkers a few blocks away

from Madame X's, who will read

your mind for nothing
on nights like these.

Her black hair,
she chopped short

sometime around the last time
she gave me bad advice.

She's always thinner than I recall,
dappling the anorexic starlet

from that popular TV comedy,
any of them.

The snow is heavy.
She's not exactly lonely,

neither am I.
I pull my Carhart

onto my sinking shoulders,
stretch on my gloves soaked

with sweat from sawing
the limbs in the driveway.

Some other force drives me out.
My fingers in wool predict

a night of bad sex
and decent whiskey,

a night drenched in the smell
of cat urine.

My boots tied. My tongue dry.
My future is at hand.

At Columbia

And Jack Kerouac came here
          to play football
then he found out he was
          a big goof
                    with a busted leg
and a library
          whose walls,
                    fortress-like,
wore names:
          Homer   Herodutus   Sophocles

I don't know why
he ever dropped out —
must have had something
          better to do!

Two Gorgeous Men on 120th Street

for Jack Burden

Milks carts
        stacked up
wear a plywood board
and on that

        a tournament,
USCF certified chess board,
        pieces,
                and clock.

The men push and pull the pieces.
        Slap at the clock.

Long coats cover them
as they perch at the edge
        of metal
                folding chairs.
A red scarf
        wraps around one
and his opponent,
        gloveless, pauses.
The only flesh to be seen
        is his hands.

A pause.
He cups the hands together
and blows into them.

Rocks forward.
Rocks backward.
Breathes into the hands
        some more.

Then the rook charges up
        the A file.
The bishop sacrifices itself
        on the 2nd rank.
The Queen stays pinned,
        the pawns locked,
and that damn rook keeps
        pressing the issue.

Pressing
and pressing.

From under the red scarf
        a howl rises,
"And I had you on time.
Man, I had you on time!"

While the pedestrians pass by,
        the pieces set themselves
back into place.
        The wind
demands the rematch.

The Chicken

The lunch crowd clambers in
from the business of suits and ties.
Splayed open chickens
fill the grill.

He's been here since breakfast
in the back booth
drinking coffee,
coffee, coffee,

thinking of their kisses goodbye —
so long and beautifully hard
he had to smell these chickens
sizzle all morning

just to warm up
to the practical sun.

IV.
The Pints

The Funeral Across from the Pub

Early A.M., sun behind fog,
soft light, blue
blue morning —
the writer walks down
six flights of stairs
to the pub.
He remembers his knees
are a bit slower
than the rest of himself
and he waits along with
the smells of damp cedar chips
for them to catch up —

      The tuba player's hat wears
      a plastic raincoat —
      He practices before the show.
            blow blow blow blow
      In the pub his crumpled uniform
            dangles on a hook.

Pictures of Michael Collins and Harry Boland cover the
wooden walls. In the corner, one frame features an article
about the brothers shot dead by Loyalists; the headline claims:
Decades Later These Brothers Haunt President McAleese.

            At some point the writer finds
            himself silly as a subject matter,

                    then all sorts of possibilities
                         stumble up to the barstool —

Across the street *Amazing Grace* played by a band of men and
women wearing naval caps and coats fills the ears of the
patrons at the pub. Plastic covers the band's suits, and the
windshield wipers make their bored motions on the hearse
now idling in front of the funeral home.

               Sitting in the pub, drinking
                    cider, Sunday morning:
                         Voyeur.

               Jimmy, the lead horn
          smokes in the doorway,
                    dancing with his cigar's haze.

While the Pigeons Sleep in their Puffy Feathers

This evening's breeze purrs slowly up the alleyway, climbing
concrete, passing dirty windows, jumping a window sill into a
7th floor apartment where the man and the woman lay under
sheets, legs touching legs, arms touching arms, hands finding
themselves wherever they will, and hair, wonderful hair:

> its smell like wet lilac
> wound with jasmine
> leaps into their chests —

The Briefly Unemployed Bouncer

He skips breakfast
as he crosses
America by bus.
Sandwich rotting
in his knapsack.

Mayo.
Bologna.
Sliced bread.
What does a fellow do
with all these things?

Creosote and ocotillo
dash by his window.
His mind is an '83
Dodge Colt.

Just to love the static again,
he dials through his channels
of beliefs, hopes, gods,
as if they were radio stations

on this interstate
heading north
from this morning's bed.

There must be a language
that doesn't depend on words;

a tuner knob that runs on clues, stray
desire, and dumb luck.

Sailing with Black Beard
for Lloyd

While working at the bar
        the other night
I met a man who
        used to be
a pirate in years past.

No patch on his shoulder.
        No parrot for a left leg.
No wooden peg over his eye.
        Still, I'll take his word
on it. It's easier that way

to snatch up some stories:
        the Filipinos
who don't bend to guns
        and aren't worth the bother;
the easy score of drug running;

tough-luck blues in arms trafficking;
        the corrupt Coast Guard as dumb
as barnacles, the more corrupt
        DEA. He speaks in breezes
while he sips beers

with a kindness in his face,
        weathered like a sail.
This kindness on his mug
        drawn from some

down deep spring.

He is old and young
        concurrently, as if
continually fished up
        fresh, like a child
sinking a fat fist

into the bottom
        of her toy box
for one more prize
        before bedtime.
He knows that the next

ship is his to claim
        and will eddy
in wait. The pirate reads
        my M. Waggener book
I left on the bar

while I clean the well bottles.
        Scanning those pages,
looking, eyes wide
        as the horizon,
he grins through a sea

of metaphor. "This guy's good,
        real good,"
he says, pushing
        the tattered book across
the brass. I wave it off.

"It's yours." He nods,
       heads out the door
into the night
       drifting through the asphalt
and the currents

of concrete
       and street lights —
the most peaceful looting
       for which anyone
could ask.

Ambition

White tennies flat
on the sidewalk,

wide palms on knees,
tired ass slumped

on the ice chest,
the hot dog salesman

rests. The sun
hides behind a cloud

to show
it aint personal.

After Last Night

I feel so good the newspaper is all Funnies —
World News: Dagwood & Blondie solve the "Violence
in Lebanon" by conducting
Couple's Communication Classes;
in *Culinary*, Hagar cures Horrible Cancer
each varietal, one after the next,
as easily as he downs
hollowed out horns filled with Mead,
Ale, or whatever you got nearby.
In *Fashion*, Dilbert keeps coats
on the backs of the poor — fixes any distribution
problem, which was his *big plan all along*,
or so he insists from behind his strategically bent tie.

One glorious,
thin page after the next
the cheap ink runs into solution, solution, solution.
In the letters to the Editor,
I dash down the mailing address
where to send
my petition to the sun
to take tomorrow off.

The Pints

Alyson walks into Chinatown,
the nearest place for cigarettes.
She leaves me to the bar and the pint glasses,
emerges onto the sidewalks

and back alleys where
she is the giant Ga-Jin
out to claim a pack of smokes —
a Welch, long-striding

concept bopping
along and along
and along —
all rhythm & ferocious hips!

A Sunny Day at the Pub Debating on Whether to See the "On the Road" Scroll at the Library or Order Another

Well, yesterday it was closed,
and the bums hunkered down
in the library doorways
while the rain showed
it meant business —
the cardboard turning
to liquid,
and the bums hunkered down.

Immortals

"Men like us should live
to be 3000 years old,"
says the man at the end
of the bar at O'Reiley's.

Dark, red lighting.
Murphy's on tap.
Powers in the shot glasses.
They drink on

as I sip away
on my beer
in the corner.
We all think,

breathe,
          breathe,
                    think.

The other man
replies, "I'd like to achieve
immortality
by not dying."

Fair enough.
          Fair enough.

V.
The United States Department of Poetry

Salvage Ethnography

Its room rectangle, long, vaguely
lit like a back alley, it's hard to know

what to make of the museum's exhibit:
"The West Explained."

A century old, the paintings of people,
of Indians, of tribes long busted up

cover the walls with the precision of
scientists, biologists, or police officers —

strict frontal, ¾ side view, profile,
a neutral grey background for all

to not detract from the study
of the figure

(name, tribe, artist, date, location
painted in red ink in the top right.)

When I step close to examine
Red Wolf, Arrapahoe, E.A. Burbank, 1898, Darlington, O.T.

the electronic voice of a woman says,
"Please step back from the exhibit."

I do. I wait. The room quiets again,

me and 126 faces

strict frontal, ¾ side view, profile,
a neutral grey background for all

to not detract from the study
of the figure.

I step back in. Get my nose
within inches of the flaked paint

on the sinewy canvas that smells
like mould, like smashed June beetles.

"Please step back from the exhibit."
I stay. I wait. We go on

like this — electronic voice,
the beetles, the tendons of the canvas, and me

not knowing what to make
of "The West Explained."

State of the U.S. Department of Poetry Report:
June 14th, 2007

The poet, the artist needs the dirt, the soil
like old Anteas, our Titan pal & great, great uncle,

needed the dirt, the soil, the earth
for it was blood! It was power.

When hoisted high in the air by Empire's
cruel champion, Herakles, whose hands are iron shackles,

when lifted by this beast,
the poet, the artist has no chance; her arms & legs

flailing at the sky, his fingers opening and closing
in the air above like a fish

in a drying lake
at the beginning of summer.

This afternoon Anthony Jayce MacDonald, descendant
of the Donegal Kings who in the eleventh century managed

to hold off the Viking hoards who inhabited Dublin,
this afternoon on Anthony Jayce's first birthday

he walks out into the backyard. He punches
one foot in front of the next, plodding

into the wild grass as high as his chest.
One foot presses down into a new wilderness;

he follows it up with the other, carrying his
newly found weight and walking muscles.

He hugs his hand around my index finger sometimes.
Doesn't sometimes. Falls sometimes.

He crouches and digs his digits into dirt,
pulls grass, picks up sticks. I walk

in front of him, tossing sharp rocks aside,
checking the grass for dryness & irritability,

finding a crushed Tecate can and pitching it
(which night was that from?)

My arm working like a slow scythe,
I sweep aside the dogs' chew bones and tennis balls.

From the deck at the top of the hill
his aunts smoke cigarettes and talk.

One of his aunt's, my wife, is a musician
with a voice that could make Odysseus

tear apart his ship's seasick planks
to hear just one more note.

His other aunt is an artist whose eyes
turn color into glass.

They watch us from above
as I, part-time accountant, take a break

from numbers and receipt books
to take this boy for a brief hike.

Concerned for his safety,
our half-coyote, half-boxer mutt sniffs

behind Anthony Jayce.
She bolts back when he turns

toward her with exploring arms
for a hug. He returns to a stick.

The dog resumes the sniffing
in the wake of his going.

I worry a bit too about his fallings,
the wires dangling from the fence

where the dog had escaped,
where I hastily reinforced with coat hangers.

But his mother is strong like the folded
& tempered steel of a sword. She has passed this

on to him. He is fearless. He is in the weeds.
I suppose it is all of our jobs to hope

the children carry on and do
something better. That they boldly

and articulately answer a mystery
for which we could barely

mouth the question.
Maybe this is the trick, the Sphinx's riddle,

the secret to the survival of one human generation
to the next, one beast, one creature to the next.

The dog now is less cautious, more
curious and gums the end of the stick

Anthony carries. They play at the idea
of tug. In the late afternoon sun

of this long lit day
an aside occurs to me. Two other artists

come to mind, Francescon & Terry,
musician and poet respectively, on break

at the auto repair shop the other day
cued me in on their conversation

on evolution. Francescon asks,
"How is it that humans survived on two legs?

Everything we fought had four legs
and their sensitive 'junk' far from the fight."

I rub my index finger over the scar
on my cheek and reply,

"Well, we made friends with the wild dogs
who ran at crotch level." They laugh.

I go on. "We fought mammoths & mastodons
whose tremendous 'junk' was at our teeth level."

Terry, as quick with his words as a squeegee with water,
rebuffs, "And the damn mammoths didn't have anything

big enough to shove tusks into." Francescon & Terry,
the Pliny the Younger & Aristotle of twenty-first century zoology

(maybe cryptology too) go back to yanking out
a cracked windshield. What do the poets,

the artists hope to do with their art?
What is it that we would want to last?

Where does all of this leave us Americans?
Us writers for the U.S. Department

of Poetry? For art rests somewhere in the soil
between sentimentality and sentiment,

buried among the rocks of sincerity and artifice.
Hard stones await our fingertips.

> Comrades, there's a baby on a hillside,
> > hunkered over and digging up something.
> A mongrel dog is wagging its furry tail in tow.
> > On this fourteenth day of June, let's crumple
> the legal papers, the notes,

those so many miscalculated spreadsheets.
Let's see what's found around the trunk
and roots of those ponderosas
in their vanilla soaked sunlight.

Timber

for Doug McGlothlin

This fall morning, soft,
lazy sunlight just now
crossing the table, falling

to the worn carpet, crawls over
a man's callused and bent
toes, feet. This light so slow

and pliable, PlayDo in the off-season
for this man, a wildland
firefighter, who shapes it

with Memory's pitted Crow's Foot;
he bangs out an anchor point,
some scratch line, flanks

an elegy for Kirk or Warren
or his grandmother perhaps,
starts containing any number

of losses, this light like clay,
orange, coarse on his fingers,
frustratingly halfway to help,

halfway solved,
halfway: like the chainsaw

running out of gas on the back-cut.

This light, he could toss it into
a woodstove all winter, and will.

Associated Press

for Alice French

The A.P. Wire of my childhood rolled back and forth printing
its dot matrix letters on connected scroll paper. In the
basement you could hear the incoming words develop into
blocks of sentences.

I'd follow my mother around the radio station, picking up
pennies that the Station Manager mis-pitched at the trash
cans. Paul Harvey, "The Rest of the Story," regularly
interrupted the day; George Straight, John Anderson, Randy
Travis repeatedly twanged from the 45s.

And down the wooden plank stairs we'd go into the
basement, like a bomb shelter, where the A.P. spit sentences
incessantly on the floor. With red pen and ruler, my mother
would stand by the Wire and lift paper from the noise.
Looked. Looked. Chopped what would be at the top of the
hour. Such power she had!

We'd climb up the creaking stairs to the News Room, leaving
all that language to revise itself, to pick its subject more
carefully next time, to come back tomorrow with better News.

Someone Must Have Quit

Highway 89:
 Bible
in the road,
  thin pages
waving
  up
      a storm
of thunderhat
clouds.

A Refrain on the Colorado Plateau
for Rick Bass

Sometime in the July morning, I hear a call from the Yaak,
and although the Yaak is a valley, the voice is a man's.

The call emerges into my world of ponderosa and plateau
through the fresh, wet-smell of morning dew.

Who knew how well the nose can listen?
As my bare feet on the concrete porch take in
        the morning's sun, the body knew,

and the call becomes
more definite, more distinct, more certain.

The followers of science conclude a human can hear, with ears,
the cry of a wolf at four or so miles. They do not know how far
        a wolf can hear a wolf,

but they've trailed a lone wolf,
perhaps a lonely wolf, roaming a range of eight hundred miles
        and finding a wolf where none was plotted to be.

How far can a human hear a human? What if we're not talking ears?
Not measuring voice like it was some horn honking?

The breath moves in slowly and out slowly and slow morning traffic
of cars and high-pitched chirps of birds and occasional scampers
        of squirrels don't diffuse the human voice to the body.

The same way the light of the morning sun overtaking the light
of the moon, low in the dark, blue-air doesn't vanquish the moon.

They are both here. The dew seeks the concrete.
The ponderosa roots below the road.

I hear a call from the Yaak, and although the Yaak is a valley,
the voice is a man's, and now the taste of my teeth
            can't be discarded;

the tongue of the snake isn't the only tongue
that can smell its way. The ponderosa a few yards past

the growing asphalt-traffic can't be left behind on the way
to a fishing hole elsewhere or a campsite on some distant
            washboard road.

My breath moves in slowly and out
slowly, and scientists still talk of *Homo sapiens*

having only five senses, but I hear a call from the Yaak
and I conclude that humans are composed of one

sense. How else to explain sky, color, light?
How else to deal with gravity, wind, the air

that moves in and out of the body and when that air
moves in slowly and out slowly forms the word?

The moon in the morning is here and the sun
doesn't make the moon doubtful. Its faith

is firm, as constant as the body receiving
the body, and so the call from the Yaak

is taken in by the body in paces, paces showing tracks
of the invisible by the expansion of the lungs,

and the return call conjured, exhaled
by the pines,
by the porch,
by the dirt,
by the road,
by the sky,
by the wind,
by this body thousands of years old
answering with breaths of light and of dark,

building slowly into the word,
building slowly into the world,

more definite, more distinct, more certain
with each assertion,
more certain with each retraction.

Grief

for Jill Divine

When she was a child
her dad used to wax
the car with lemon pledge —
gobs and gobs of it —

so she could slide
and slide along
its slick aerodynamics.
Memories like that might help.

Freddy Arizona and the Trains

for Wade Dorffi

He limps. You'd expect that.
Legs bowed like lodge pole pines

that somehow got the mind they wanted
to go for a stroll.

For Freddy Arizona has been hit by the train
four times.

Survived each time,
every time.

No one knows if it's the same
train each time, every time, except

for a handful of teary eyed conductors
or maybe Freddy Arizona himself.

Hit four times by trains — Freddy A Z,
the miracle of the Copper State!

Freddy presses on.
His right shoulder jutted up

like a big idea about to be birthed;
his jaw fused tight

as a statue waiting

to whistle a tune.

For our man Freddy has been hit
by more than four trains.

The running count: two taxi cabs;
one tourist in a long truck fresh off the lot;

six drunken bicyclists, all in parade-like sequence,
after the bars closed.

Disability? You said it.
He collects from everyone:

VA Benefits,
lawsuits against the State for which he's named,

Federal suits,
asbestos filings,

and the checks roll in
and he cashes them

and cashes them:
the tired currency of his pains,

the capital of his wrecks.
He cashes them

as reliably as arthritis
and windy winters.

They run a route
into his dented, old mailbox.

And he scoops them out,
totes the bills over to the taverns,

to the pubs in downtown, in old town.
And for this, of course, Freddy Arizona catches

lots of fists, especially in the firsts
of the months when the cash is fresh.

You find him detoured, delayed in alleys,
pants pockets ripped out

or sprawled on the sidewalks
by the kicked-in newsstands;

slouched into a fresh black eye,
busted nose scabbing up.

Freddy Arizona has been hit by the train
four times; survived each time,

every time. The fists
while frustrating for Freddy

don't add up to much
in the scheme

of his world where entire states
wear his name. Freddy

Arizona will be there
each first to collect the next

and the next.
Tonight, I sit and drink, sit and stew

and miss Freddy. It's impossible
to feel sorry for yourself

or anyone else when Freddy Arizona
flops onto the barstool beside you,

and, besides, I owe
his hide at least a beer

or four. As now,
so do you.

Notes

"Baelnablath": The epilogue is from Levis's poem "The War" from *Wrecking Crew*.

"Golems": The poem refers to the golems of the Old Testament that were built into an animated statue-like being out of the materials of a region. They were typically a force of righteous retribution.

"Pulling Down the Sky: A Report": The Czeslaw Milosz quote is taken from his book of prose poems, *Road-side Dog*.

"Salvage Ethnography": The West Explained exhibit is in the Butler Art Museum in Youngstown, Ohio.

"Today Lets Call Ourselves Ghalib": Inspired in Prescott by a poetry reading from Miles Waggener and a photo gallery display by Matt Hammon, I used thoughts on creativity and the arts from both artists in order to fuel this poem. Ghalib is an Indian poet who Robert Bly translated into English in the book, *The Lightning Should Have Fallen on Ghalib*. I was lost in that as well that day. Ghalib's wonderful lines and boldness made me wish I could be as confident in my own poetry, my own observations and decisions. I'd rather be Ghalib than God any day of the week.

Acknowledgments

I would like to thank Sean Carswell, Jill Divine, and Thor Nolen for their continual feedback on these poems. Also, I'd like to thank Mark Gibbons and Miles Waggener for their inspiration and close reading of this book as a whole. And thanks to Alyson Jay who provided the music.

I'd like to thank the editors of the following journals where some of these poems first appeared.

Alligator Juniper, "Today Let's Call Ourselves Ghalib"

Flag Live, "Timber," "Sailing with Black Beard"

Moon Reader, "Someone Must Have Quit"

International Studies of Literature and Environment (ISLE) Journal, "Refrain on the Colorado Plateau"

Strange Machine, "The Fourth of July County Fair Donkey Speaks," "Sympathy for Jesus"

Poets of the American West, a Many Voices Press anthology, "Mars Hill"

About the Author

James Jay has worked as wild land firefighter, book seller, surveyor, and furniture mover. He lives in Flagstaff, Arizona where he has taught poetry at the jail, the public schools, and the university. His poems and essays have appeared in numerous journals and magazines. He received a MFA from The University of Montana and a MA in Literature from Northern Arizona University. Currently, he is a columnist for *FlagLive*, the Executive Director of the Northern Arizona Book Festival, and owns a bar, Uptown Billiards, with his wife, Alyson.